C000183498

Losing

a Pet

Losing
a Pet

COPING WITH THE DEATH
OF YOUR BELOVED ANIMAL

Jane Matthews

Published by:

Published and distributed by:
small books
21 Station Terrace
Great Linford
Milton Keynes MK14 5AP, UK
Tel: (044) 1908 670080
Email: info@smallbooks.co.uk
www.smallbooks.co.uk

Book design by:
More Than WORDZ - www.morethanwordz.co.uk

Front cover picture by Becky Browne
Back cover picture by Jane Matthews

A catalogue record for this book is available from the British Library

ISBN 978-0-9556643-0-4

Printed in China

ACKNOWLEDGEMENTS

Many thanks to Paul Manning of Astonlee Veterinary Surgery, Newport Pagnell, who not only cast an expert eye over the text but shared some useful insights from his own veterinary practice.

I am also grateful to Yvonne Cook, for her useful suggestions on the first manuscript and for gentle editing. And to Nikki Zalewski who has been far more than the designer of this book, a source of ideas and, even more importantly, of belief in its value.

Finally, the booklet could not have been written without input from the many pet owners who shared their memories, thoughts – and sometimes photos too – in the hope that they would help others.

DEDICATION

To Amy, who came up with the idea
for this book, and to my good friends
Shushie and Cheska for being there.

CONTENTS

Chapter 1

LIVING WITH A PET

Our pets are what turn our houses into homes.

Whenever I've been away, whether it's for a few hours or for a long holiday, it's my cats I most look forward to seeing again; more than the bricks and mortar, or the garden or the letters on the mat.

At the end of the day, when I collapse in the chair with a cup of tea and my thoughts, it's my pets I want alongside: easy, companionable, happy to let me be me.

And when I'm upset, it's they who instinctively know to come and show me I'm adored!

AN OPEN HEART IS A VULNERABLE HEART

But the moment we choose to keep a pet we make ourselves vulnerable. Even if our cat or dog or pony or rabbit lives to an old age then the chances are we'll still live longer. And, sadly, many of them don't live out their full lifespan, but are taken early from us by illness, or in accidents, or they simply disappear and we never know where or why.

We know our pets are not people, but that doesn't stop our hearts breaking when we lose them.

Losing a pet can be every bit as shattering, every bit as traumatic, as any other bereavement.

◀ **Mutz by Shirley Paley**

SUFFERING IN SILENCE

Because such losses are rarely written or talked about, we are often unsure whether to discuss them, not trusting others to understand the depth of our pain. Instead, we suffer in silence.

The one thing in our life that has always been there for us when we are grieving is the very reason we are so inconsolable. Without any obvious way of sharing our pain, it can feel as if it is almost too much to bear.

A TALE OF FIVE CATS

Most animal lovers suspect that it is their pets who chose them rather than the other way around. That was certainly true for us when one Saturday morning someone rang the doorbell and ran away.

But the doormat wasn't quite empty. On it sat a cardboard box and nestled inside was a mother cat and her four kittens.

The mother was a short-haired tabby, painfully thin. Her eyes looked hollow and sad, in contrast to her kittens, whose eyes were still tightly shut to this new world they had suddenly landed in.

Two of the kittens were long-haired tabbies, the smudgy colour of soot. The third had short hair like its mother, only several shades of smoke lighter. The fourth kitten was the colour of an apricot, its long hair curling from its soft belly.

To this day we have no idea who brought the cats, nor why they chose our entirely ordinary, terraced house.

But what a wonderful favour they did us.

Princess – named by the children for the day she turned up, just after the Princess of Wales had died – and her small brood dug themselves into the house, into the furniture, and into our hearts. By the time two months had passed and, with it, the date the RSPCA told us the kittens would be weaned and they could take them off our hands, we were besotted – and determined that we would find a way of ensuring we could still see the little creatures who had snuffled and poked and purred their way into our lives. The little apricot cat, now called Marmalade, went to our babysitter, while the light tabby, who'd inherited his mother's big sad eyes, went to an uncle who named him Scrumpy.

We called the two long-haired kittens Pocket and Tails and found a willing home for the male, Tails, with an aunt. Pocket, we decided, should stay with her mother – and with us.

LOVE AND LOSS

Just like *your* pets, ours brought us so much joy and fun and loving companionship over the years. They were part of the family and so, so easy to love and enjoy.

And when my uncle died, it was an obvious thing to do to bring home again the little tabby we'd boarded out to him. Scrumpy may not have been a favourite with his mother and sister, who clearly resented having to share us with an interloper, but we loved having him back.

Ten years have passed since they arrived. Two years ago we lost Princess, most likely to a car.

She managed to make it home but died of internal injuries.

And now Pocket has joined her. Our dear, irrepressible Pocket, so full of character and love it seemed such a small body could hardly contain it.

Pocket, too, died as a result of a car. Too many people travelling too far and too fast: the precise opposite of our pets whose whole presence serves to slow us down, relax us, and remind us that however mad the world is, it is affection and friendship, the deep peace that comes from loving and being loved, that makes life worthwhile.

That turns our houses into homes.

YOU AND *YOUR* BELOVED PET

If you are reading this because your pet has died I am so very, very sorry for your loss. And I know that, at this moment, it may feel as if the grief will never end; that you will never be able to remember the good times you shared without every memory bringing you right back to your sadness.

In your grief may you find some comfort in this short book; in the experiences of others who may not have known your wonderful companion but know something of what you are going through.

In the recognition that this is not a small loss and that there is nothing unusual or wrong about the depth of your feelings.

And in the practical help and support offered, in the spirit of friendship, to help you get through the weeks to come.

**Wilbur by
Kate Smith** ▶

Chapter 2

WHEN A PET DIES

"One of the worst things about Sam dying was not being able to talk to anyone about it. I knew if I said anything at work people would look at me as if I was a bit crazy. I just couldn't explain how huge it was to have lost him. I ended up staying home for a week rather than go in and have people wonder why my eyes were so red." **Terry**

Bereavement is a common experience. None of us will go through life without losing *someone* we care about.

When a friend or relative dies the people we know expect us to be upset. They understand and usually show their sympathy by being kinder and tolerant if we are distracted or emotional.

There are agencies to help us deal with bereavement, and books and services set up to support us. Workplaces have arrangements in place for compassionate leave. There are sections in every card shop where people can choose a message to tell us they understand our grief and grieve with us.

Many of us experience losing a pet in the same way as we would any loved one. We are floored; as grief struck as we would be at the loss of any friend or family member.

And yet we may not know where to look for support with *this* loss. Worse, we may fear that some of those closest to us will respond with bafflement, incomprehension, impatience, even humour – not meant nastily but only adding to the feelings of isolation which bereavement can bring.

MIXED EMOTIONS

Indeed, it's quite common for pet lovers to describe experiencing some of those feelings of bafflement themselves. We may wonder why our emotions are so powerful, get angry and impatient or defensive and apologetic for being so upset, or for taking so long to 'snap out of it'.

Nor is it unusual to feel guilty and embarrassed: embarrassed that we are reacting so strongly to the loss of an animal, when so many of our fellow humans are suffering so much on a daily basis; guilty that the emotions we're feeling may even seem stronger and more raw than for other bereavements involving a relative or friend.

After all, we know when we take on a pet that it's unlikely to outlive us. We will most likely have to face up to its loss at some point.

One of the reasons I decided to write this book was to reassure you that whatever you're feeling, however you are experiencing this tremendous loss, you have no need to feel guilty or embarrassed or apologetic.

There are no league tables when it comes to bereavement. Losing a pet can feel every bit as awful as losing a person and, slowly, our society is coming to acknowledge this.

Increasingly, bereavement and counselling agencies are recognising that how we grieve when we are bereaved depends not on the number of legs or strength of the blood ties, but on what the one we've lost meant to us. And your pet may well have meant the sun, the moon and the stars to you.

"It's been 12 days since that terrible night and everyone thinks I should be back to normal, but how can I be normal when my life is upside down? I hate coming home. I feel as if my heart is broken."
Sandra

WHY DO WE FEEL SO STRONGLY?

Their love is unconditional

You have every reason to grieve. Our pets are special. Yours was.

If you think about it, for most of us there are only two times in our lives when we are loved unconditionally.

As babies, we come into the world and are greeted with love, delight, indulgence, and full-on attention.

Parents, relatives, friends, neighbours, flock to visit and admire us, tell us how proud they are when we smile or make a sound. It is a heady feeling to be loved and accepted for exactly who we are.

And one we may never entirely experience to the same extent again in our lives – until we have a pet who honours us with the same total, unconditional love and acceptance.

Our pets tolerate our moods, our bad days and bad tempers, our foibles and eccentricities and they do not waver in the depth of their love.

That's a huge thing to lose and can leave us feeling as if an anchor has been slashed and we have been cast adrift.

We feel responsible
The comparison with babies is important for another reason: whether or not we have experienced parenthood ourselves, we understand how it is to be small and vulnerable.

As pet owners, we are very aware of our animals' vulnerability and may consider ourselves in a role similar to that of a parent, taking care of them because they are unable to fully understand our world. Like babies, they cannot speak to tell us what they fear and what they need and what puzzles them.

That relationship, based on their trust, leads to a very special kind of love. And to an awareness of responsibility that may, when we lose our pet, make us feel we have let them down in some way – especially if their death was due to accident or illness. Should we have loved them more? Looked after them more? Protected them more than we did?

They let us be ourselves
With our animal companions we never have to explain ourselves. We never have to be anything other than what and who we are.

We will never find our pet judging us for being ourselves, or for what we've been or done or said.

They are part of the fabric of our daily lives

"I work from home so we were together all the time. I wake up and expect to see her laying by the bed. I take a shower and expect to see her by the bathroom door when I come out. I look under the desk to make sure I won't kick her when I shift my feet. I save scraps from my plate for her. I never realised how much a part she was of every day." **Joanne**

If we are animal lovers the chances are our pets will have been a part – and in some cases the reason – for those life-enhancing moments when we are most relaxed or at peace. They have become part of the fabric of our homes and families so that we cannot imagine a mat without them on it, a garden chair which we don't have to fight them for, or waking up in the morning without a soft nose nudging at us to go and sort out some breakfast.

It is hardly surprising that the space they used to occupy can seem so vast. Many of us see more of our pets on a day-to-day basis than many of the people in our lives, however important to us those people might be.

REMEMBER YOU ARE NOT ALONE

If you have found yourself quietly nodding at some of those reasons why your grief is so intense then you must know that you are not alone. However lost and isolated you might be feeling at this moment, there are millions of others who have loved and lost a cherished animal and know what you are going through.

Over the page, you'll find some suggestions for places to turn to and ways of sharing your feelings and your loss with others who'll understand and may help you through the grieving process.

Burying your feelings may help you get through the day to day, especially immediately after your loss, but it can prolong your grieving in the end. Whereas sharing your thoughts, feelings and memories aloud with a sympathetic listener can help you heal.

Like many other big emotions, grief and loss take their own course and dictate their own timetable. Let them. The way we experience bereavement is as individual as our pets themselves.

Talking it through

- It is almost always helpful to talk but you need to find someone who'll be sympathetic and won't find the depth of your emotion strange.

- The staff at your local veterinary practice have huge experience in helping pet owners deal with loss, even if a few days or weeks have passed. Don't be scared to contact them and ask what services are available to help you – or simply if you can go in and talk to someone.

- Similarly, your local doctor's surgery will be able to put you in touch with the nearest bereavement counselling service in your area if you feel you want professional support.

- Trusted friends and family will want to help but sometimes they may be finished with your grief long before you are finished with your need to talk about it. You need to find an understanding, non-judgmental listener with whom you can openly acknowledge your feelings and talk about the happy times for just as long as you need to.

- You could try sharing your thoughts with other pet owners who will almost always understand. Don't be surprised if you find sympathy in some unlikely quarters: many other people in your acquaintance have never had the chance to open up either.

- Alternatively, you could phone one of the pet bereavement lines in the back of this book.

- Or visit a pet website (addresses for these are also in the back) and post a tribute or join an online chat or support group.

- You could book a session with a counsellor in your area: the Citizen's Advice Bureau or library should be able to give you a contact.

- Animal charities are another place to find like-minded people who will be sympathetic.

- Remember, you don't have to explain yourself to anyone if you don't want to. Saying you've suffered a bereavement but feel unable to talk about it is usually enough to stave off enquiries from people who you suspect won't understand.

Reggie and friend by Becky Browne ▲

Chapter 3

LIVING THROUGH LOSS

In the same way that no two dogs, cats, ponies or guinea pigs are ever quite the same, nor is the way we respond to loss.

It's this very fact that we *do* experience loss so differently from each other – in our own way and our own time – that can make us feel so alone. Yet there are patterns and stages to loss and being aware of those will help you recognise them and face up to them when they arrive.

UNDERSTANDING HOW LOSS WORKS

As you contemplate what you've lost it is useful to remind yourself of a few things.

Firstly, the grief that is caused by losing something we love seems to be experienced cumulatively.

Whereas with an emotion like anger we may feel it, express it, deal with it, and move on, we seem to struggle to let go of loss completely. We learn to live with it, but at some level, however deeply buried that is, the losses we've experienced as we've gone through life are still with us.

So as you mourn the loss of your beloved pet it is quite normal for a whole lot of other losses and bereavements to come flooding back and add to the power of what you're feeling: from your parents splitting up or your grandparents dying, to other pets you may have lost.

You can't help that, so acknowledge your feelings, allow yourself to have them, and accept your need to mourn – and celebrate - all over again the things you've loved and lost.

And that's the second point to remember. The thing to do with feelings is feel them.

We don't choose our feelings. They are the body's way of connecting us to ourselves, cutting through the busyness of day-to-day life to alert us to what is going on and what we need to pay attention to.

LOSS IS A ROLLER COASTER

"The early weeks were the most painful for me. By then the shock which helped to numb the pain had worn off. And the sad reality set in. After that my grief came in rolls, like waves on an ocean shore. Sometimes not so bad, other times raging like a storm. I realised all I could do was roll with it."
Zara

Loss is best described as a roller coaster, hurling our emotions up and down so fast we can feel we have no control over them.

We may think we're beginning to come to terms with our loss then a few moments later find we are choked with tears because someone has said a kind word, or because something has reminded us that our pet is no longer there.

Feeling out of control is uncomfortable and stressful and it's tempting to want to try to over-ride our pain by focusing on other things, throwing ourselves into work, or DIY, or numbing ourselves with too many alcoholic drinks or shopping sprees – anything to distract us.

But feelings are nature's way of enabling us to deal with loss and heal from loss. So it's vital not to try and short circuit them – not to jump from the moving roller coaster in other words. Accept that you will have good days and bad days and there is often no way of knowing in advance which will be which.

Bottling up your feelings, telling yourself they're unwanted or unacceptable, is a bit like stuffing the cork in a fizzy bottle. In the end they'll almost certainly find another way out – and the resulting explosion could end up hurting you or others even more.

GIVE YOURSELF TIME

Remember that sooner or later – however impossible it seems right now – time will begin its healing process. That doesn't mean you won't still be sad sometimes when you think about your pet and the wonderful times you shared together.

Clichés become clichés because they are true: time may not fix things but it does heal. Your pain won't be as intense as this for ever. Think about other times in your life when you were really unhappy, perhaps as a child when someone hurt you or you were really anxious about something. Now you look back, you can see your feelings are no longer so strong. They've passed and you've survived and learned and grown a little.

Emotional hurts may not be visible to us in the way a wound is but it's useful to think about them in the same way: treat your hurt as you might an injury, with care and kindness, and with patience, knowing that if you do so your body will begin to mend itself. The wounds that don't heal and become troublesome are the ones that are ignored.

Healing yourself

- Take time off from your normal daytime routine. We're very good at insisting 'life must go on' when, actually, it doesn't always have to. Taking time out is a way of acknowledging the depth of your loss.

- Make your healing your priority. That means putting your needs above other people's for a while. So if there are things you don't feel like doing then give yourself permission not to do them.

- Treat yourself with the same love and compassion you'd give a friend: that means sympathy, care and attention. No beating yourself up or pushing yourself.

- From a practical point of view TLC means as much sleep as you need, long soaks in the bath, a walk in the sunshine: anything that brings you peace or the sense you are nurturing yourself.

THE STAGES OF LOSS

Remember we are all different so you won't necessarily go through all these stages, or even go through them in this order. But it's helpful to know any of these feelings, below, are quite normal, and just about every other human being on the planet will experience them at some time – you are not alone.

Shock and denial – why us?

Whether you knew your pet was dying or would need to be put down, or the death came out of the blue, it's very normal to go through a period of almost disbelief. You may feel as if you're on 'auto-pilot', going through the motions, unable to feel anything much at all.

Some people even experience a false 'high', getting on with things as if nothing had happened, a stranger to themselves and their emotions.

Shock and denial are nature's anaesthetic, a way of getting us through those first, awful days of unbelievably raw pain. And if you're the kind who normally copes with everything life throws at you and likes to be in control you may be particularly susceptible to slipping into a period of numbness or disbelief.

Jaffa and Phoebe by Katherine Davison ▲

If you can't believe it's happened, or can't connect with your feelings, don't add to your load by getting anxious about this response. Be certain that nature knows best. Everything happens in its own time and when you are ready to deal with these big emotions you will start to feel them.

Needing to make sense of loss

Along with shock may come the feeling that life is unfair, that bad things ought not to happen to good people and wonderful pets. You want an explanation, want to understand how this could have happened, and why it happened to you and your beloved animal.

Sometimes we feel that until we are able to understand, to find a reason 'why?', we'll be unable to move on.

There are two kinds of needing to know. The first is about knowing the circumstances and is an entirely normal part of bereavement – just one we tend not to acknowledge because as a society we've tried to airbrush the reality of death out of the picture. There is nothing sordid or macabre about wanting to know as many details as you can. For many of us it is an important stage in enabling our mind to process what has happened.

On the other hand, the bigger question about why this particular set of circumstances has happened to you and your pet is the one that may have your thoughts chasing themselves endlessly and futilely around your head.

As with every other stage in your grieving journey, try to treat yourself gently. Sometimes in life there are answers and explanations; often there are not. Your pet lived very much day-to-day, not regretting the past or anticipating the future, and there's a lesson for you in that.

It's those who learn to accept that life can be chaotic and unfair, but who allow themselves to love and be loved anyway, who find peace the soonest.

Anger and blame

These feelings sometimes go along with strong feelings of anger and a need to blame someone: we look for an outlet, somewhere we can vent emotions we fear may overwhelm us. Perhaps the truth is that someone *was* to blame, but nothing will bring your pet back. And getting angry with whoever you blame – especially yourself – will only add to your hurt. If a lesson needs to be learned from what happened then make sure it is. But don't allow yourself to get stuck in blame. A good outlet is to write a letter expressing all your feelings, then rip it up or burn it in order to let those feelings go.

If anger is your main emotion you need to find a physical outlet: find somewhere private where you can shout and scream or thud a pillow, or smash a few plates, or walk as though your life depended on it. Anger is a physical emotion and it needs to be expressed through intense activity. You *will* find that bit by bit you feel a little better as you allow yourself to unload your anger safely, without harming yourself or those around you.

"It was hard enough losing Rusty. I'd had her from a pup. What made it worse was that I blamed Mike for her getting run over. I was away on a course and it was his job to look after her. He knew I thought it was his fault so there was all this guilt and blame and anger between us and we ended up not speaking for several weeks. I can see now that made it even harder. We both loved her so we ought to have been the best people to help each other, instead of which we both retreated into our own worlds." **Marilyn**

Guilt

Perhaps you feel you should have loved your pet more, looked after it even more carefully than you did, never got impatient when it wanted food or a walk or just attention and you were busy with something else?

Guilt is another very common emotion when we are going through loss. It's as if we feel that unless we suffer along with them we couldn't have loved them enough. Our guilt is a kind of penance.

Yet we already are suffering in our loss. While our dear pets are not feeling pain any more; nor can they be hurt. All our feelings of guilt are doing is adding more layers to the sadness we're already feeling.

And one thing you can be certain of, guilt and blame are not feelings our pets would recognise.

Tell yourself you did the best you could. We all spend so much of our lives trying hard to get things right. You were doing the best you could at the time and knowing what you did then.

The pit
As we said, we rarely experience feelings of loss and grief in a straight line. Just when you think you might be able to look at a picture of your pet again without crying you stumble on an empty pet bowl in the cupboard and start to

howl. You can hardly believe that after all this time and all these tears the grief seems as real and as strong as ever.

It almost certainly won't be, however, and once you've dried your eyes you can take a step back and acknowledge that it's taken you a little less time to recover than it did during the first few days of your loss.

The exception to this is when grief subsides into a kind of permanent heavy heartedness, as if the world has turned grey and you wonder in the mornings what there is to get out of bed for.

If this happens to you and you realise that there are no signs you're beginning to move through grief then your loss may have triggered depression and it would be sensible to seek professional help from your doctor.

There's nothing to be ashamed of; human beings can be very complex and one set of emotions triggering another is not unusual.

Acceptance

Reaching this point doesn't mean you've stopped feeling sad, but the extremes of emotion should be behind you. You won't be thinking about your loss all the time and not everything will remind you of your missing pet. It's important to tell yourself that reaching the stage where you accept your loss is not a betrayal of your pet. Pets bring us such joy, and they love to see us happy. That's why we keep them.

Giving and receiving love is the greatest gift this planet has to offer us and you have experienced that. In time you'll want to celebrate what you brought to your pet's life, and what he or she brought to yours.

"I think we all want to be loved and remembered when we die, but we also want to know that the ones we left behind are doing alright without us – because we love them so much. Now I can see that because my pet loved me so much being strong is one of the ways I can return that." **Jonathon**

▲ Anna with Indiana and Bonnet the kitten
by Mike Goodman

Chapter 4

PRACTICALITIES

"It was the children who asked if we were going to have a funeral and even though it was emotional it helped me as well as them. I let them arrange everything and I suppose afterwards there was a feeling of relief, of lightness." **Jenny**

By the time you read this you may already have made the decision about whether your beloved pet is to be buried or cremated, whether the ashes are to be returned, or not.

You don't need permission to bury your pet in your garden, but it can be a hard thing to do, bringing home the reality of your loss. For that reason, many people now choose cremation. There are pet crematoria in every region and all local vets will be able to direct you to the nearest one, or arrange the cremation for you.

When they do so you will be asked whether you want an individual cremation – so that your pet's ashes can be returned to you. Or a simple communal cremation, which will mean the ashes can't be returned. If you opt for individual cremation you will be asked which casket you want – your choices will range from a simple cardboard box to carved and decorated wooden caskets – and whether you want the ashes returned to you or buried at a pet cemetery.

COMMEMORATE AND CELEBRATE YOUR PET

Whatever you decide, you may well feel you want to do something more to commemorate your loss, and to celebrate the dear friend your pet was to you. There's no need to be embarrassed about that. For centuries those who could afford it set up little pet cemeteries close to their homes: there's scarcely a stately home without its own pet graveyard. In our age, as we've come to recognise the importance of our pets in our lives, a number of companies have begun to offer pet memorials of every style and price – from a simple memorial note on a pet lover's website to a full-blown granite headstone.

The important thing to remember is that making arrangements to commemorate your pet is actually far more about you than about them. Thinking and planning how we want to celebrate our pets keeps us busy and gives us a focus for the myriad of emotions we are experiencing. So be sure to make choices that feel right to you rather than worrying about doing things in the way you think they 'ought' to be done.

In exactly the same way that preparing a funeral for a friend or relative helps us gather our thoughts, remember what they meant to us, and allows us to feel we are carrying out a final act of caring, so too does making those same arrangements for our pet.

We are demonstrating what they meant to us and performing an act of service to show our gratitude to them for all that they contributed to our lives.

FUNERAL FOR A FRIEND

Unlike funerals for people, your pet funeral can take any form you like. It may be no more than a short prayer or reading a poem at the bottom of the garden. Or you may want to invite friends who knew and loved your pet too. You may want to organise music, a tribute, readings – or all of those things.

It can be nice to ask those who knew and loved your pet to write down or read out a memory of a time you all shared, and for you to do the same. You can collect them together in a small book.

If you struggle to express your feelings in words, find a poem or song that resonates with you. At the end of this booklet are a few suggestions for poems and readings. You can also find poetry and suitable thoughts on some of the websites listed in the resources section.

Music for remembering

You will have your own favourites – and it's possible your pet did too! But, if not, here are some suggestions you may like

- The Circle of Life from The Lion King (Elton John)
- Let it Be (The Beatles)
- Over the Rainbow (Judy Garland and others!)
- Fields of Gold (Eva Cassidy)
- Fly (Celine Dion)
- Bright Eyes (Art Garfunkel)

A PLACE TO REMEMBER

You may want your pet's body, ashes or memorial close by in the garden, or, if you don't have space, somewhere your pet loved to go: a favourite haunt or walk that you both enjoyed visiting. Alternatively, your vet or nearest pet crematorium can advise on what choices you have. Most crematoria have a garden of remembrance where you can place a memorial, or a book of remembrance where you can write your thoughts or include a photograph. You can pay for a stone or entry in the book of remembrance at the crematorium if you wish.

The advantage of erecting a stone or creating a special place for your pet is that you have somewhere real where you can go and remember.

You may not feel the need for that: many people say they can sense their pet in and around the home the way they always were. But it can be consoling to create a special place of remembrance, for instance by planting a rose tree or other shrub or flower, erecting a stone, or perhaps a bench or seat where you can sit and feel grateful to have had your pet's love.

If you don't have room, you could approach your local parks authority for permission to plant a tree or place a bench in tribute to the hours you and your pet shared there.

Many vets surgeries keep noticeboards for pictures of pets, or a book of remembrance where you can write down your thoughts or a special tribute. If your local surgery doesn't have a book yet try suggesting the idea to them – you'll be doing a service to other pet owners.

A tribute to your pet

There are plenty of other ways to pay tribute to your pet, which may also benefit other animals:

- sponsor an animal at a rescue centre or zoo
- make a donation to an animal charity
- organise a sponsored event to support a relevant charity
- volunteer some time to help at an animal sanctuary
- create a scrapbook of photos and memories
- commission a painting from a photograph of your pet
- name a star for your little star!
- post a tribute to them on one of the pet memory websites.

And don't overlook the obvious – a favourite picture for the wall, which will remind you of the fun and love you shared; and give you the chance to tell stories and remember what made your pet such an individual.

LIVING WITH UNCERTAINTY

One of the cruellest fates that can befall any animal lover is to have their pet disappear.

We imagine the worst. But so long as there is no news, no sign, no body, we are left hanging in a kind of limbo, unable to start mourning but equally unable to get on with anything else.

It is absolutely normal at such times to experience all the same stages of loss, but added to them may be an inability to concentrate, feelings of being lost or stuck, or a sense of everything else in your life being on hold. You may have phoned every vet in the area, put up signs and adverts, combed the roadsides and parks and hammered on shed doors looking for your pet, yet you still feel completely helpless. As if your fate is out of your own hands.

Here too it will help to talk to others who've experienced a pet's disappearance by contacting one of the places listed in the resources section. Don't feel as if you can't because you don't know whether your pet is alive or dead: they will have spoken to many others in the same boat and will want to help you.

Miracles happen. Our animals do find their way home to us. They do turn up bedraggled and skinny from some adventure we can only guess.

But you can only deal with living in limbo for so long; sooner or later, if your pet does not come home, you need to give yourself permission to accept they have gone – in order that you can fully experience the stages of loss and grieving and, finally, moving forward again.

You owe it to yourself and to those who care about you, including your missing and much loved pet.

Amy and Princess ▶

THE GREATEST LOVE

"I could not watch him suffer any more as I knew he was suffering for me. Putting him to sleep was the most difficult decision I've ever had to make and I've questioned my decision over and over again. Is there something more I could have done? Should I have kept trying? I know I did the right thing for him, but it feels so wrong. I just have to find comfort in knowing he is no longer suffering." **Beth**

It may be that you have picked up this book because you are facing one of the toughest decisions we can be asked to make: whether to have your pet put to sleep.

What makes it tough is not only anticipating such a huge loss, but the confusion of knowing when is the right time to make the decision.

You love your pet: it's absolutely natural that you want to do everything in your power to help them if there is a chance they can get well again or least have a good quality of life during a prolonged illness.

And yet there will come a time when your vet, your pet through its behaviour, or your own instincts, tell you it is time to let go.

You need to know that giving permission for your pet to be put to sleep is not a failure on your part but an act of huge compassion and courage. You are putting its peace of mind, its need to move to the next stage in the circle of life, ahead of your own need to be with your pet. Euthanasia actually means 'gentle death'.

When that moment comes think hard about what you need to do to make such a difficult time as easy on you both as possible in the circumstances. Perhaps you want the vet to come to you? Perhaps you want it to be a time when you know you can take a few days to recover, for instance at the end of the week or when you have few commitments?

If your pet is already at the surgery is it kinder to leave it there or bring it home? If the operation is performed at the surgery is there someone who can come and support you? Can the vet give you time alone with your pet afterwards? Do you need someone to drive you home in private?

When to let go
Is your pet:

- Suffering from pain, distress or serious discomfort which can't be controlled with medication?
- Is it having difficulty walking or balancing?
- Finding it difficult to eat and drink enough without vomiting?
- Suffering from tumours which cause pain and are inoperable or untreatable?
- Having difficulty breathing?
- Incontinent or having difficulty urinating or defecating?
- Behaving in ways that are totally out of character?

If you've answered yes to any of these the time may have come to consider whether you need to let go.

"I know a lot of people feel guilty about having their pets euthanised but they should think how they might feel if they hadn't. I'm still haunted by the memory of how ill Sky was before I called the vet out to him and if I could change things now I think I would have called the vet earlier, although I really did what I thought was best for him at the time." **Yvonne**

Archie by Tracy Buchanan ▲

Chapter 5

LIFE AFTER LOSS

The sadness of your loss may never leave you completely but, in time, the pain of it will lessen. You may only think about your pet from time to time, when a word or object or place reminds you of the missing face in your life. And many of those thoughts will be happy ones; good memories of times you shared.

If this doesn't happen and, after a few months, you still find yourself often in tears then you may need to seek professional help, either from a counselling agency or a special bereavement service – see the resources section for suggestions.

As the pain fades from the almost unbearable to an occasional heartache, there is no need to feel guilty about this. Your pet loved to see you happy. As humans we don't keep animals to add to our load but to enjoy and cherish. You did not take your beloved pet on in order to feel sad but to love and be loved and you can continue to do that even though your pet is out of sight.

NO REPLACEMENT

One of the first things people will ask you, or suggest to you, is that you should get another animal.

But keeping a pet is not like replacing a light bulb. You need time to grieve, time to adjust, and time to assess, before you consider whether to take such a significant step.

It's quite normal to feel for a while that you never want to put yourself in the position again where you may lose something you love.

But such feelings usually pass. One of the wonderful things about the human heart is that there is no limit on the love it can contain. Just because you are ready to love another pet takes nothing from the love you feel for the pet you lost. We have an endless capacity to love: just ask anyone who keeps six, sixteen or sixty animals!

Sometimes we feel guilty all over again, as if getting another pet is in some way a betrayal of the pet we lost. In reality it's the opposite. It's precisely because we loved our pet so much – and got so much back – that we want to do it all over again.

And just think what joy you bring to an animal's life. Your love is a gift to your pet, as surely as your pet brings pleasure and love to your life.

Honey and Henry by Nikki Zalewski ▲

Resources

WEBSITES AND OTHER ORGANISATIONS THAT CAN HELP

Blue Cross
Support line: 0800 096 6606
Email: pbssmail@bluecross.org.uk
www.bluecross.org.uk

The Blue Cross runs a pet bereavement support service via telephone or email. You'll be able to talk to a trained volunteer befriender who will understand what you are going through. You can also post a tribute to your pet in a special memorial area of the Blue Cross's website.

Cruse Bereavement Care
Helpline: 0844 477 9400
Email: helpline@cruse.org.uk

www.crusebereavementcare.org.uk
Cruse has lots of information on bereavement in general that you may find helpful.

www.petsavers.org.uk
Petsavers is a charity funding studies into the diagnosis and treatment of sick pets. Its website features a section where bereaved pet owners can submit pictures and words about their pet.

www.petloss.com
This website carries tributes, poems and stories from those whose pets have died; visitors to the website are encouraged to contribute their own and to take part in a global Monday evening candle ceremony to remember pets. The website also hosts a chat room, has links to other useful websites and telephone lines, and posts relevant articles.

www.chancesspot.org
Another good American site with publications to download, an area for tributes, a weekly online support group, and some fun stuff too!

Association of Private Pet Cemeteries and Crematoria

Tel: 01252 844478

www.appcc.org.uk

The Association offers advice on the type of services available and has a search facility to help you find a suitable provider. Its database includes a small number of crematoria which can deal with horses.

POETRY AND READINGS

The readings and poems in this section are from a range of sources and are offered simply as suggestions or starting points as you make your own choices, depending on your own beliefs and circumstances.

Extract from Ecclesiastes 3.1-8

To everything there is a season, and a time to every purpose under the heaven: a time to be born and a time to die; a time to plant, and a time to pluck up that which is planted…a time to weep and a time to laugh; a time to mourn and a time to dance.

Do not stand at my grave and weep

I am not there. I do not sleep.
I am a thousand winds that blow.
I am the diamond glints on snow.
I am the sunlight on ripened grain.
I am the gentle autumn rain.
When you awaken in the morning's hush
I am the swift uplifting rush
Of quiet birds in circled flight.
I am the soft stars that shine at night.
Do not stand at my grave and cry;
I am not there. I did not die.

What is Dying?

A ship sails and I stand watching
'til she fades on the horizon, and
someone at my side says, "She is gone".
Gone where?
Gone from my sight, that is all.
The diminished size and total loss of
Sight is in me…and just at
The moment when someone at my side says
"She is gone," there are others who are
watching her coming,
And other voices
Take up a glad shout, "There she comes!"
And that is dying.   *Bishop Brent*

Something beautiful

The tide recedes, but leaves behind bright
seashells on the sand.
The sun goes down but gentle warmth still lingers
on the land.
The music stops, and yet it echoes on in sweet
refrains.
For every joy that passes, something beautiful
remains.   *Author unknown*

Rainbow Bridge

Just this side of heaven is a place called Rainbow
Bridge.
When an animal dies that has been especially
close to someone here, that pet goes to Rainbow
Bridge.
There are meadows and hills for all of our special
friends so they can run and play together.
There is plenty of food, water and sunshine, and
our friends are warm and comfortable.
All the animals who had been ill and old are
restored to health; those who were hurt or
maimed are made whole and strong again, just as
we remember them in our dreams of days and
times gone by.
The animals are happy and content, except for
one small thing; they each miss someone very
special to them, who had to be left behind.

They all run and play together, but the day comes when one suddenly stops and looks into the distance. His bright eyes are intent; his eager body quivers. Suddenly he begins to run from the group, flying over the green grass, his legs carrying him faster and faster.

You have been spotted, and when you and your special friend finally meet, you cling together in joyous reunion, never to be parted again. The happy kisses rain upon your face; your hands again caress the beloved head, and you look once more into the trusting eyes of your pet, so long gone from your life but never absent from your heart.

Then you cross Rainbow Bridge together....

Author unknown

The Heart

What the heart has once known, it shall never forget.   *Anonymous*

Charlie by Vanessa Leslie ▶

ABOUT THE AUTHOR

Jane Matthews is an award-winning journalist and author of a series of self-help books on making better relationships and on surviving life as a carer. She is also an accredited Heal Your Life teacher. See www.lifechoiceslifechanges.co.uk for workshop details.

FORTHCOMING TITLES
FROM SMALL BOOKS

- The one book on self-esteem you need

- How great are you? Self-esteem for teens

- Inside Affairs